E S T A T E   P U B

GRIMSBY · CLEI

IMMINGHAM · HOLTON LE CLAY · HU

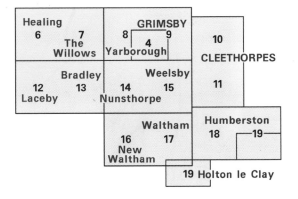

5	Immingham

- Healing **6**
- The Willows **7**
- **8**
- GRIMSBY Yarborough **4** **9**
- **10** CLEETHORPES
- Bradley **12** **13**
- Laceby
- **14** Nunsthorpe
- Weelsby **15**
- **11**
- Waltham **16** **17**
- New Waltham
- Humberston **18** **19**
- **19** Holton le Clay

ROAD MAP   pages 2-3

ENLARGED CENTRE   page 4

INDEX TO STREETS   pages 20-24

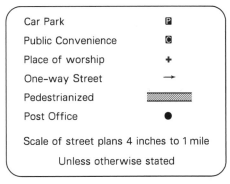

Car Park   P

Public Convenience   C

Place of worship   +

One-way Street   →

Pedestrianized

Post Office   ●

Scale of street plans 4 inches to 1 mile

Unless otherwise stated

Street plans prepared and published by ESTATE PUBLICATIONS, Bridewell House, Tenterden, Kent, and based upon the ORDNANCE SURVEY mapping with the Permission of The Controller of H.M. Stationery Office

The publishers acknowledge the co-operation of North East Lincolnshire District Council, and East Lindsey District Council in the preparation of these maps.

ISBN 0 86084 781 0

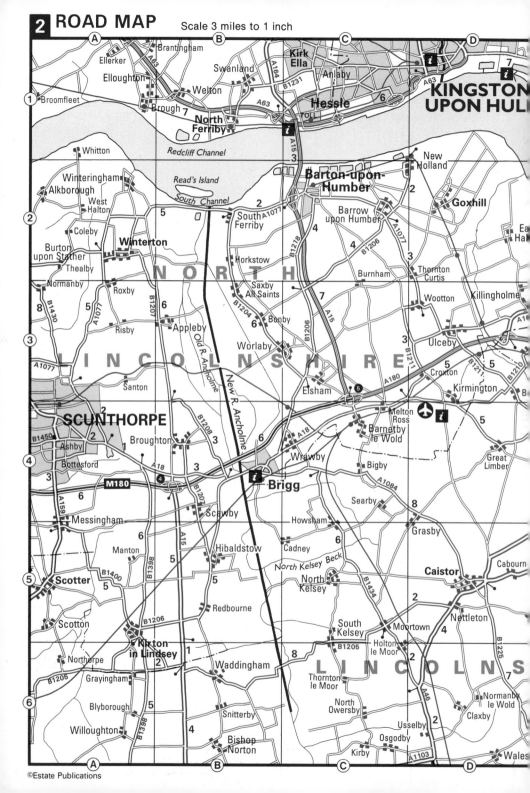

2 ROAD MAP

Scale 3 miles to 1 inch

©Estate Publications

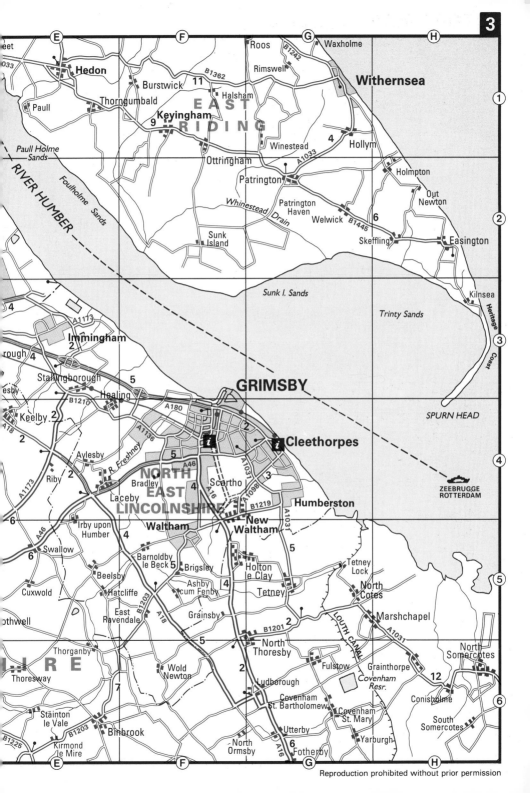

E F G H

Roos
Waxholme
B1242
Rimswell
Hedon
B1362
Withernsea
Burstwick 11
Halsham
① 1
Thorngumbald
Paull
E A S T
Keyingham 9
R I D I N G
Hollym
Winestead
4
Ottringham
A1033
Holmpton
Patrington
Paull Holme
Sands
Patrington
Out
Haven
Newton
Whinestead Drain
Welwick
6
RIVER HUMBER
B1445
② 2
Foulholme Sands
Sunk
Skeffling
Easington
Island
Kilnsea
Sunk I. Sands
Trinty Sands
4
Heritage
A1173
③ 3
Immingham
2
rough
Stallingborough
5
SPURN HEAD
Coast
sby
B1210
Healing
GRIMSBY
Keelby 2
A180
A18
A1136
Cleethorpes
2
i
2
North
i
④ 4
Riby 2
5
ZEEBRUGGE
EAST
Scartho
ROTTERDAM
Bradley
A46
A1173
Aylesby
A16
LINCOLNSHIRE
4
Humberston
R. Freshney
B1219
6
Laceby
A1031
Irby upon
New
Humber
4
Waltham
Waltham
Swallow
Tetney
6
Barnoldby
Lock
Beelsby
le Beck 5
Brigsley
North
Cuxwold
5
Holton
Cotes
le Clay
⑤ 5
A46
Ashby
cum Fenby
4
Tetney
Hatcliffe
Marshchapel
A1031
East
North
B1203
Ravendale
Grainsby
Somercotes
othwell
A18
LOUTH CANAL
12
Thorganby
5
2
North
Grainthorpe
Conisholme
Thoresway
Wold
Thoresby
Fulstow
Covenham
South
Newton
7
Resr.
Somercotes
2
Covenham
Stainton
Ludborough
St. Bartholomew
⑥ 6
le Vale
B1203
Covenham
Binbrook
St. Mary
Kirmond
A16
Utterby
Yarburgh
B1225
le Mire
North
Ormsby
6
Fotherby
E F G H

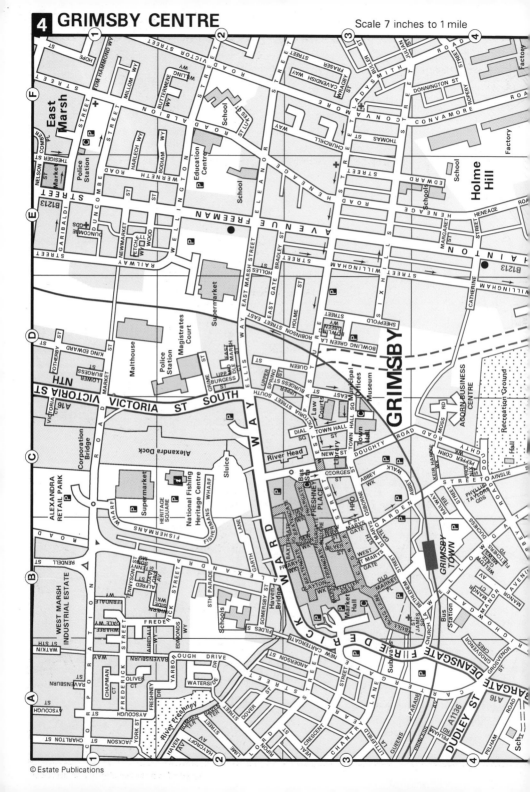

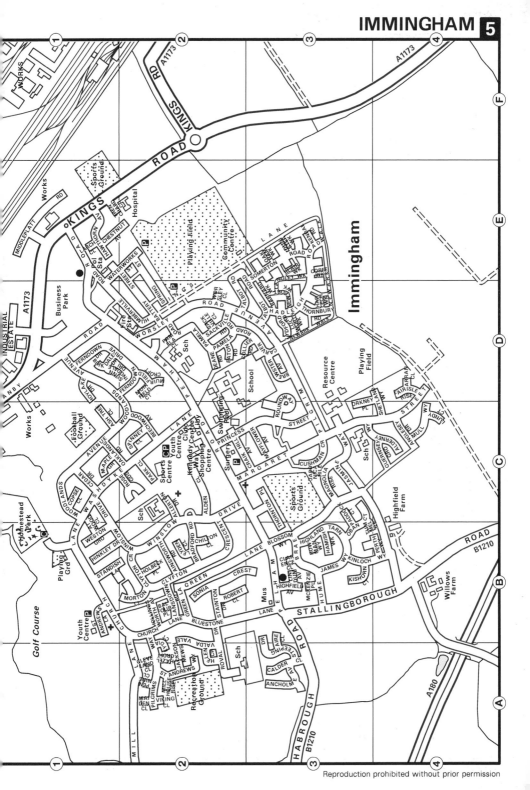

Immingham

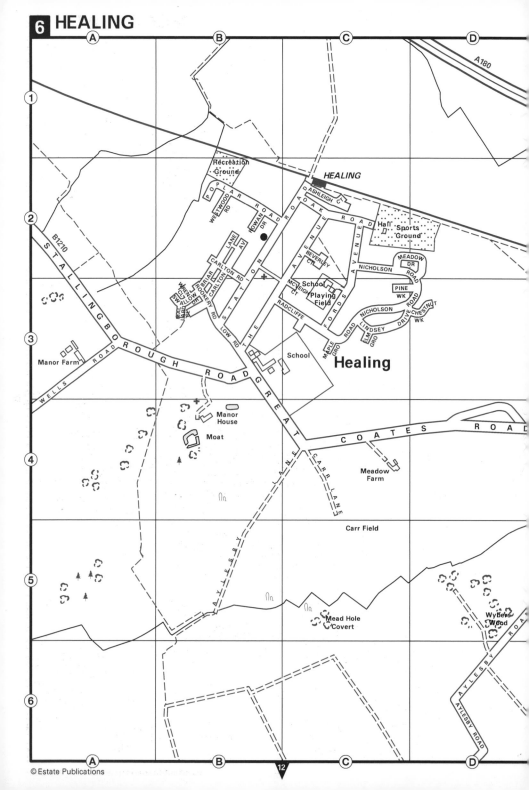

HEALING

Healing

A180

B1210

STALLINGBOROUGH ROAD

GREAT COATES ROAD

Recreation Ground

POPLAR ROAD

WESTWOOD RD

ROWAN DR

OAK AVENUE

AVENUE

OAK ROAD

ASHLEIGH CT

Hall

Sports Ground

MEADOW DR ROAD

NICHOLSON

PINE WK

BEVERLEY CT

CARLTON RD

CARLTON LANE

BRIAR LANE

ROOKERY RD

SWALLOW WALK

MALLARD

AV

STATION ROAD

LOW RD

THE

MCVEIGH CT

School Playing Field

RADCLIFFE

MAPLE GRO

FORDS ROAD

ELM GRO

LINDSEY GRO

NICHOLSON

CHESTNUT WK

DRIVE CHESTNUT

Manor Farm

WELLS ROAD

School

Healing

Manor House

Moat

AYLESBY LANE

CARR LANE

Meadow Farm

Carr Field

Mead Hole Covert

Wybers Wood

AYLESBY ROAD

AYLESBY ROAD

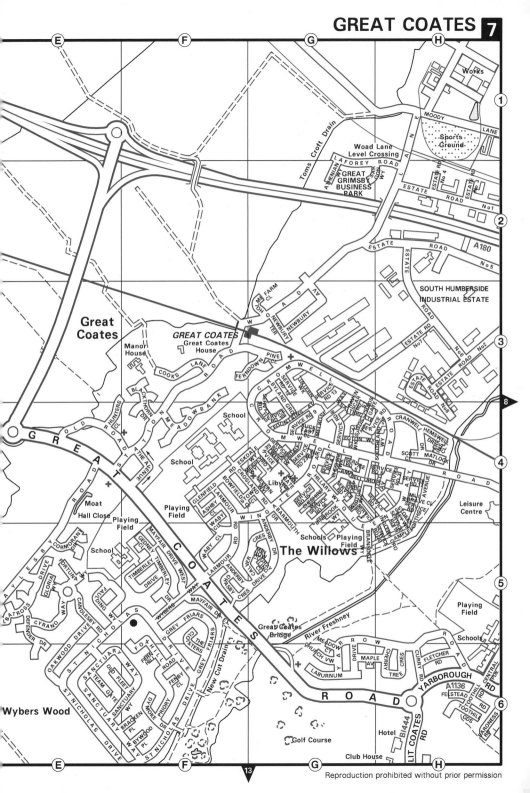

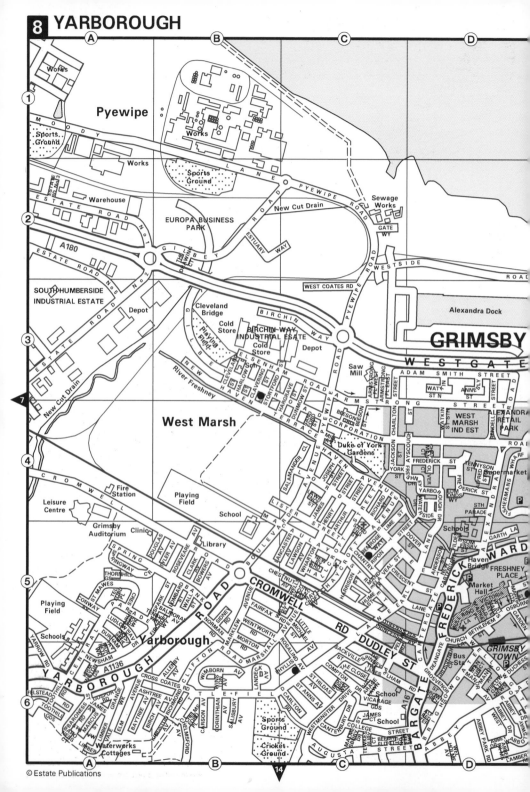

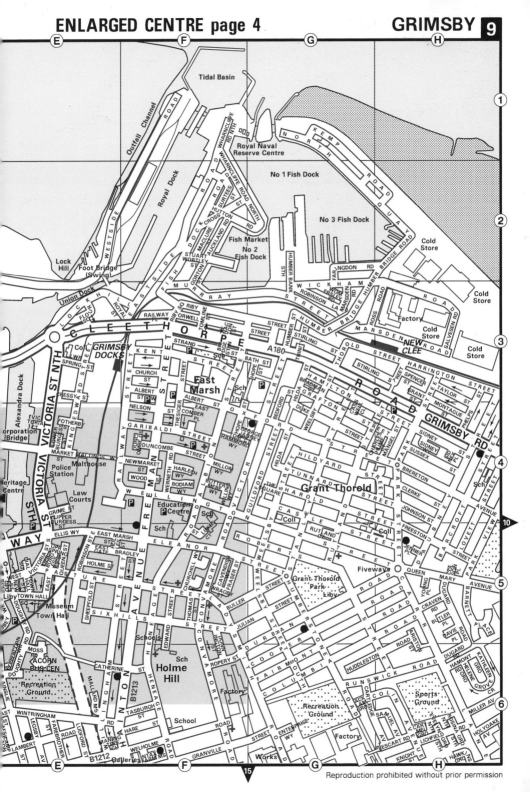

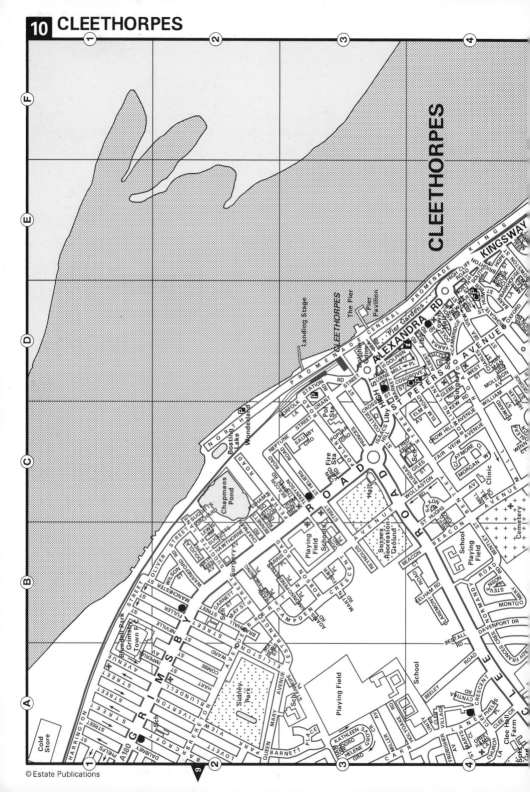

CLEETHORPES

KINGSWAY

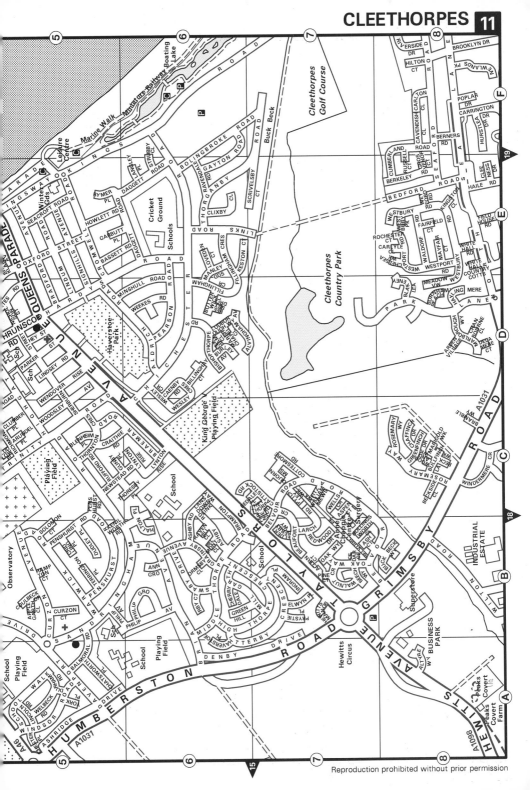

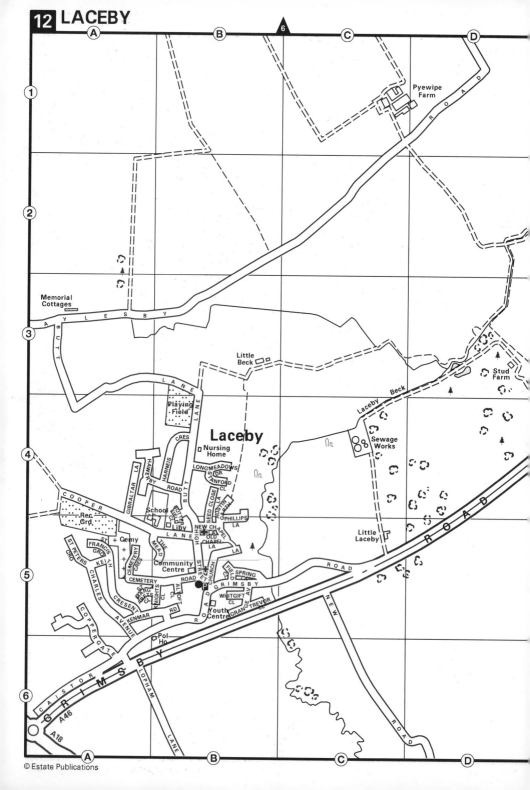

12 LACEBY

Pyewipe Farm

ROAD

Memorial Cottages

A Y L E S B Y

B U T T

Little Beck

Stud Farm

Laceby Beck

LANE

LANE

Playing Field

Laceby

Nursing Home

Sewage Works

CRES

HARNEYS

ABBY

GIBRALTAR LA

COOPER

Rec. Grd.

School

LONGMEADOWS
DR
ANFORD
CL

BUTT LANE

SEED CLOSE

KIRKBY
CL

AUSTIN
LA

PHILLIPS
LA

Little Laceby

ROAD

ELLIE
MEAD

Liby

CEMETERY CRES

NEW CHAPEL
OLD
CHAPEL
LA

CL

LA

ROAD

ST PETERS
CRO

FRANCIS
GRO

KEL

CRESENT

CEMETERY

Community Centre

GRIMSBY

SPRING

CHURCH STREET

KNIGHTS
CL

ALTOF
CL

WHITGIFT
CL

GRANGE AV

TREVOR

Youth Centre

Cemy

CHARLES

AVENUE

KENMAR

COPPERGATE

Pol. Ho.

NEW
ROAD

C A I S T O R

G R I M S B Y

A46

A18

CLOPHAM
LANE

© Estate Publications

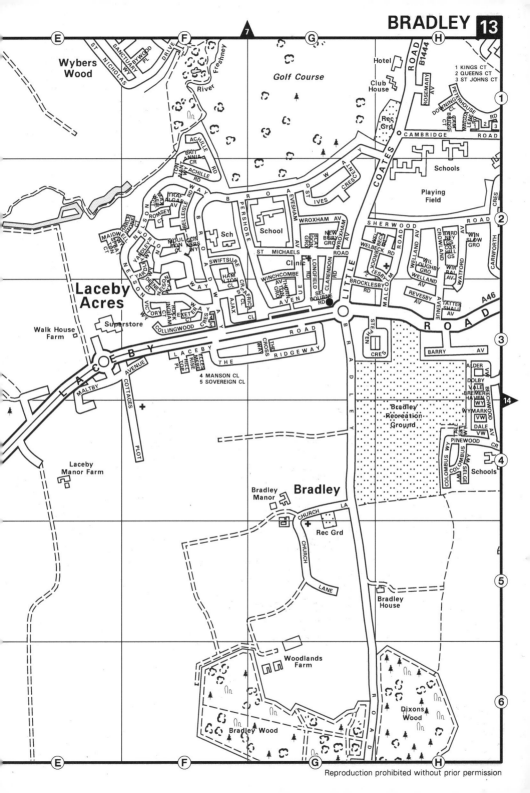

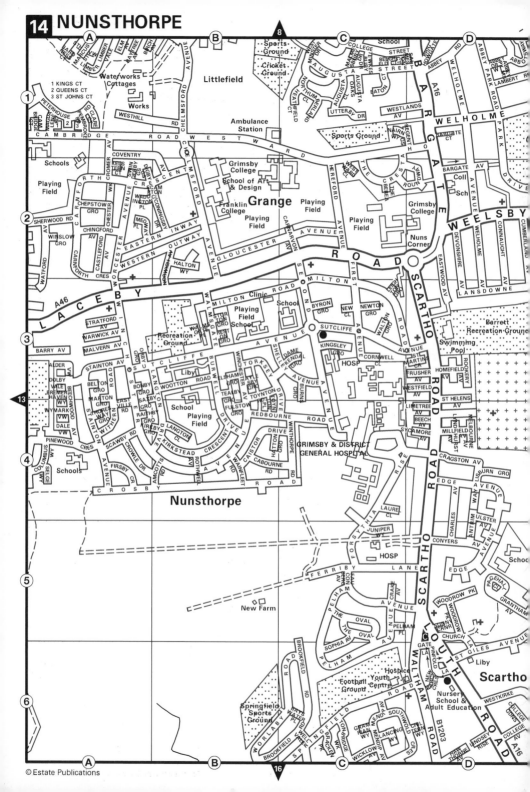

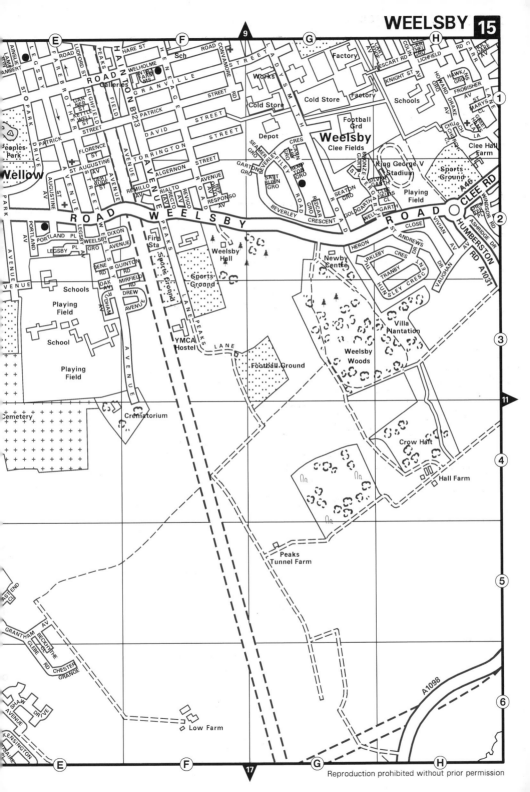

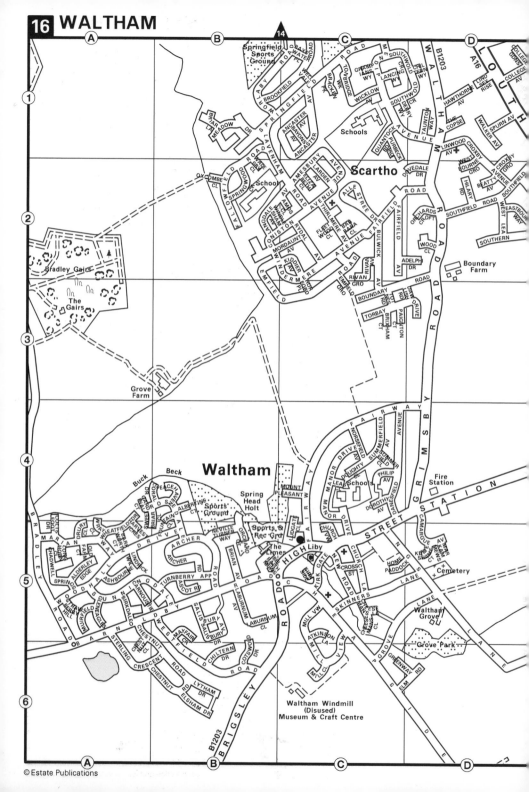

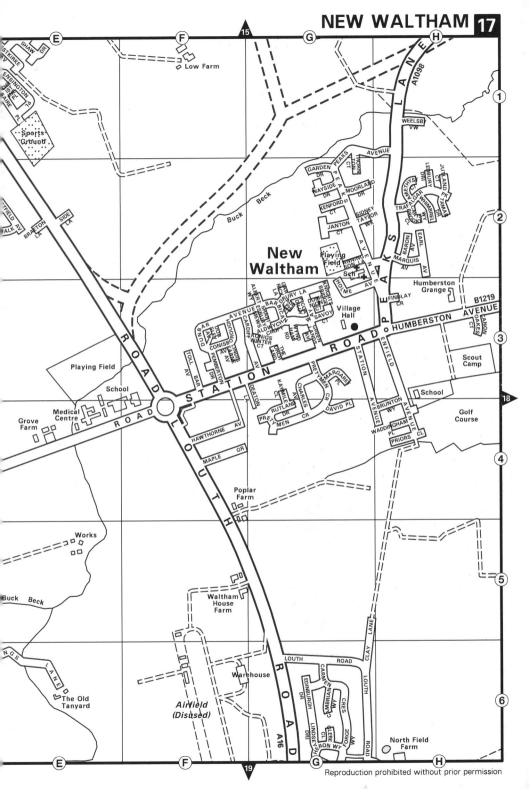

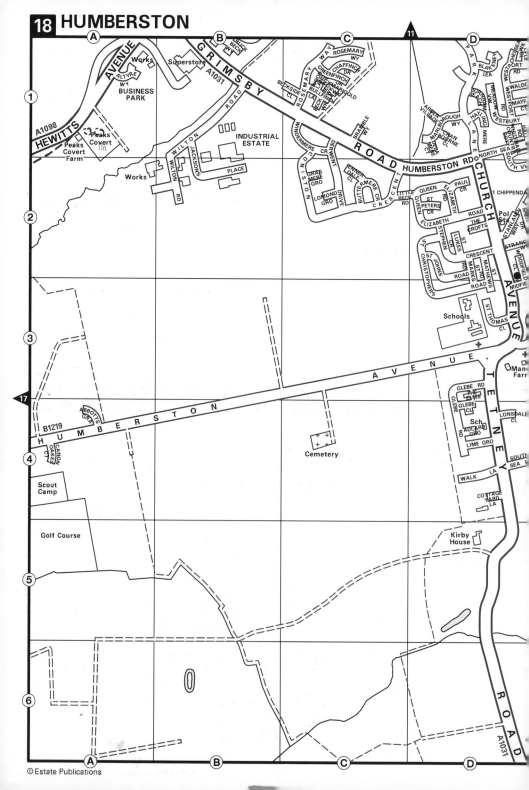

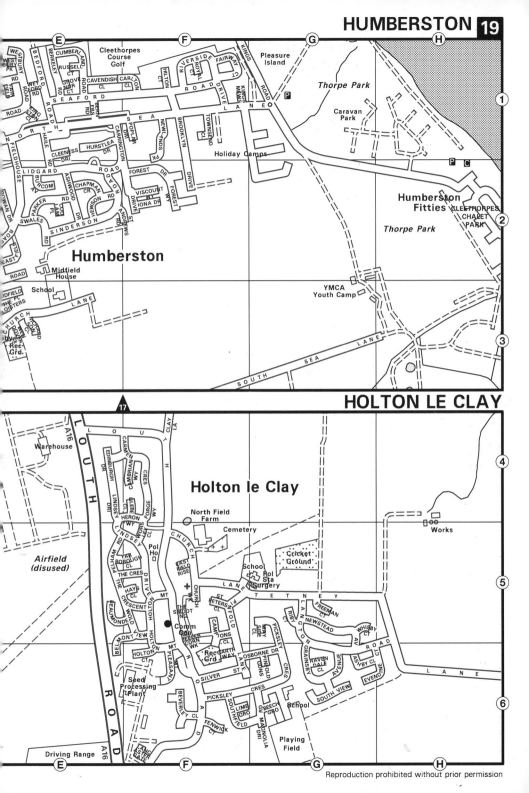

HOLTON LE CLAY

The Index includes some names for which there is insufficient space on the maps. These names are preceded by an * and are followed by the nearest adjoining thoroughfare.

GRIMSBY/CLEETHORPES

Street	Ref
Abbey Dri East. DN32	8 D6
Abbey Dri West. DN32	8 D6
Abbey Pk Mews. DN32	8 D6
Abbey Pk Rd. DN32	8 D6
Abbey Rd. DN32	8 D6
Abbey Wk. DN31	4 C3
Abbotsway. DN32	8 D6
Abbotts Grange. DN36	18 A4
Achille Rd. DN34	13 F1
Acklam Gro. DN32	9 G6
Acorn Business Centre. DN31	4 C4
Acorn Ct. DN35	11 B7
Adam Smith St. DN31	8 D3
Adams Rd. DN35	10 B3
Adelphi St. DN36	17 G3
Adelphi Dri. DN33	16 D2
Adlard Gro. DN36	18 D4
Africa Clo. DN34	13 F3
Ainslie St. DN32	9 E6
Airedale Way. DN31	4 A1
Ajax Clo. DN34	13 F3
Albatross Dri. DN37	7 E5
Albert Rd. DN35	10 D4
Albert St East. DN31	9 F3
Albert St West. DN32	9 F3
Albert Way. DN36	17 G3
Albertine Ct. DN37	16 B4
Albion St. DN32	4 F1
Alder Vw. DN33	14 A3
Alderley Edge. DN37	16 A5
Aldrich Rd. DN35	11 D6
Aldwych Croft. DN36	17 G3
Alexandra Retail Pk. DN31	4 C1
Alexandra Rd. DN31	4 B2
Alexandra Rd. DN35	10 D3
Alfred St. DN31	4 B1
Alfred Ter. DN32	8 D6
Algernon St. DN32	15 F2
Allenby Av. DN34	8 B6
Allestree Dri. DN33	16 C2
Altoft Clo. DN37	12 B5
Altyre Way. DN36	11 A8
Alvingham Av. DN35	11 D6
Amcotts Rd. DN34	14 B4
Amesbury Av. DN33	16 C2
Amethyst Ct. DN36	17 H2
Amos Clo. DN33	16 C2
Ampleforth Av. DN37	7 H5
Ancaster Av. DN33	16 C1
Anderby Dri. DN37	7 F5
Anderson St. DN31	4 A3
Ann Gro. DN35	11 B6
Annesly St. DN31	8 D4
Annington La. DN36	17 G2
Antrim Way. DN33	14 D5
Applegarth Clo. DN35	11 B5
Archer Rd. DN37	16 B5
Arden Village. DN35	11 D8
Ariston St. DN32	9 H5
Armstrong Pl East. DN31	8 C3
Armstrong Pl West. DN31	8 C3
Armstrong St. DN31	8 C3
Arthur St. DN31	8 C5
Arundel Pl. DN35	11 C5
Arundel Wk. DN34	8 A5
Ascot Rd. DN37	16 B5
Ash Ct. DN35	11 B7
Ashbourne. DN37	16 A5
Ashby Clo. DN36	19 G6
Ashby Clo. DN37	7 F4
Ashby Rd. DN35	11 B6
Ashleigh Ct. DN36	6 C2
Ashridge Dri. DN35	11 A5
Ashtree Av. DN34	8 A6
Ashwood Dri. DN36	19 E2
Aspen Ct. DN35	11 C7
Athenian Way. DN37	7 G2
Atkinson La. DN37	16 C5
Auckland Rd. DN31	9 F2
Augusta Clo. DN34	14 C1
Augusta Oaks. DN34	14 C1
Augusta St. DN34	8 C6
Austin Garth. DN37	12 B4
Aylesby Gro. DN33	14 B3
Aylesby La. DN37	6 B5
Aylesby Rd. DN37	7 E5
*Aylesby Wk, Torksey Dri. DN33	14 B3
Ayscough St. DN31	4 A1
Bader Clo. DN37	7 G4
Balmoral Av. DN34	8 B5
Balmoral Rd. DN35	11 A5
Barbara Clo. DN37	16 C2
Barbican Way. DN36	17 G3
Barcroft St. DN35	10 A2
Bardney Gdns. DN34	13 H2
Bargate. DN34	8 D6
Bargate Av. DN32	14 D2
Bargate Ct. DN32	14 D1
Bark St. DN35	10 D4
Barkhouse Clo. DN35	10 E4
Barkhouse La. DN35	10 D4
Barkworth Ct. DN37	16 A5
Barmouth Dri. DN37	7 G4
Barnett Pl. DN35	10 A2
Barnoldby Rd. DN37	16 A5
Baron Av. DN36	17 H2
Baroness Rd. DN34	8 A6
Baroness Ct. DN34	8 A6
Barry Av. DN34	13 H3
Bassett Rd. DN35	11 E5
Bath St. DN32	9 G3
Baxtergate. DN31	4 B3
Bayons Av. DN35	16 C1
Bayswater Pl. DN33	16 C1
Baytree Av. DN34	8 A6
Beacon Av. DN35	10 B4
Beacon Ct. DN32	9 G3
Beaconthorpe Rd. DN35	10 C3
Beatty Av. DN32	16 D2
Beaufort Cres. DN35	11 B7
Beaumonde. DN36	19 E5
Beck Wk. DN35	11 C8
Beckhythe Clo. DN33	15 E5
Beckside Clo. DN35	11 C8
Bedale Pl. DN35	11 C7
Bedford Rd. DN35	11 E8
Bedford St. DN32	9 G4
Beech Av. DN33	14 D4
Beech Gro. DN36	19 G6
Beech Way. DN35	11 B7
Beechfield Ct. DN34	8 C6
Beechwood Av. DN33	14 A3
Beeley Rd. DN32	10 A4
Beesby Dri. DN35	11 D6
Beeson Gro. DN31	8 C4
Beeson St. DN31	8 C4
Belleisle Rd. DN34	13 F2
Belmont. DN36	19 F5
Belmont Clo. DN35	11 B6
Belraith Mews. DN37	16 B5
Belton Gro. DN33	14 A3
Belvoir Pk Wk. DN37	11 B7
Belvoir Rd. DN35	11 B7
Bempton Gro. DN32	15 G2
Bemrose Way. DN31	8 C5
Bennett Rd. DN35	10 B2
Bentley St. DN35	10 B4
Berkeley Rd. DN35	11 E8
Berners St. DN31	11 F8
Bestall Rd. DN32	10 B4
Bethlehem St. DN31	4 B4
Beverley Rd. DN35	19 F6
Beverley Ct. DN37	6 C2
Beverley Cres. DN32	15 G2
Billinghay Cres. DN35	11 D6
Binbrook Way. DN37	7 G4
Birch Av. DN34	8 B6
Birchin Way. DN31	8 C3
Birchin Way Ind Est. DN31	8 B3
Birkdale. DN37	16 A5
Bishops Wk. DN34	8 C6
Bishopthorpe Rd. DN35	11 D6
Blackthorn Dri. DN37	7 F4
Blakeney Lea. DN35	11 C7
Blaydon Gro. DN34	13 G2
Blenheim Pl. DN35	11 C5
Blundell Av. DN35	10 A2
Bodiam Way. DN32	4 E2
Bolingbroke Rd. DN35	11 E6
Bonby Gro. DN33	14 A3
Boulevard Av. DN31	8 B5
Boundary Rd. DN33	16 C3
Bowers Av. DN31	8 B5
Bowfield Clo. DN37	7 F4
Bowling Green La. DN32	4 D3
Bowling Green Way. DN32	4 D3
Bowling La. DN35	10 C4
Bracken Pk. DN33	16 C1
Bracken Pl. DN37	7 F6
Bradford Av. DN35	11 D5
Bradley Rd. DN37	13 G3
Bradley St. DN32	4 E2
Bradman Ct. DN32	9 G3
Braemar Rd. DN35	11 C6
Braeton La. DN33	17 E2
Bramble Way. DN35	11 C8
Bramhall St. DN35	10 B2
Brampton Way. DN35	11 B6
Bransdale Way. DN37	7 G5
Bremerhaven Way. DN33	14 A3
Brereton Av. DN35	10 A2
Brewery St. DN31	4 B3
Brian Av. DN35	11 A6
Brian Av. DN37	16 B5
Briar La. DN35	16 B1
Briar La. DN37	6 B3
Bridge St Nth. DN32	9 F3
Brighowgate. DN32	8 D6
Brighton St. DN35	10 E4
Brigsley Rd. DN37	16 B6
Britannia Cres. DN34	13 F1
Brixham Ct. DN33	16 C3
Broadfield Rd. DN33	14 B6
Broadway. DN34	13 F2
Brocklesby Pl. DN34	13 H2
Brocklesby Rd. DN34	13 G3
Bronzegarth. DN32	15 G2
Brookfield Rd. DN33	16 B1
Brooklands Av. DN35	11 E5
Brooklyn Dri. DN36	19 F1
Browns Orchard. DN32	4 D3
Brunton Way. DN36	17 H4
Buck Beck Way. DN35	11 B8
Buckfast Clo. DN37	7 G4
Bull Ring La. DN31	4 B3
Buller St. DN32	9 F5
Bullfinch La. DN35	11 C8
Bulwick Av. DN33	16 C2
Burcom Av. DN36	19 E2
Burley Av. DN35	11 D6
Burnham Reach. DN35	11 B8
Burns Gro. DN33	14 C3
Bursar St. DN35	10 C4
Burwell Dri. DN33	14 B3
Butler St. DN35	9 H5
Butt La. DN37	12 A3
Butterfield Clo. DN37	12 B4
Buttermere Cres. DN36	18 C2
Buttermere Way. DN32	4 F2
Butterwick Clo. DN35	11 D6
Byland Clo. DN37	7 G3
Byron Gro. DN33	14 C3
Bywood Pl. DN37	7 F6
Cabourne Rd. DN33	14 B4
Caenby Rd. DN35	11 D6
Caistor Dri. DN33	14 B4
Caistor Rd. DN37	12 A6
Calver Cres. DN37	7 G5
Camargue Av. DN37	16 D5
Cambrian Way. DN36	19 F4
Cambridge Ct. DN34	13 H1
Cambridge Rd. DN34	13 H1
Cambridge St. DN35	10 D4
Campbell Gro. DN37	7 G4
Campden Cres. DN35	10 B3
Campions Clo. DN37	19 F5
Candlesby Rd. DN37	7 E5
Canon Oakes Ct. DN36	18 A4
Canterbury Dri. DN34	8 C6
Cardiff Av. DN36	17 G3
Cardinal Ct. DN37	16 A4
Carisbrooke Clo. DN36	17 H2
Carlton Av. DN37	6 B3
Carlton Clo. DN35	11 F8
Carlton Rd. DN34	8 C6
Carlton Rd. DN37	6 B2
Carlyle Clo. DN35	11 E8
Carmen Cres. DN37	19 F4
Carnaby Gro. DN32	15 G1
Carnarvon Av. DN34	14 C2
Carnforth Cres. DN34	14 A2
Carnoustie. DN37	16 A5
Carr La. DN35	9 H5
Carr La. DN37	6 C4
Carrick La. DN36	17 G3
Carrington Dri. DN36	19 E1
Carson Av. DN34	8 B6
Cartergate. DN31	4 A4
Cartledge Av. DN32	9 G6
Cartmel Gro. DN32	9 H6
Casswell Clo. DN32	9 G4
Castle St. DN32	9 G4
Castleford Av. DN34	14 A2
Catherine St. DN31	4 D4
Cattistock Rd. DN35	11 C7
Cavendish Clo. DN35	11 B8
Cavendish Way. DN32	4 F3
Cedar Clo. DN35	11 B7
Cemetery Cres. DN37	12 A5
Cemetery Rd. DN37	12 A5
Central Par. DN34	8 A6
Central Prom. DN35	10 D3
Chadwell Springs. DN37	16 A5
Chaffinch Dri. DN35	11 C8
Chantry La. DN31	8 C5
Chapman Ct. DN31	4 A1
Chapman Cres. DN32	19 E2
Chapman Gro. DN35	10 B2
Chapman Rd. DN35	10 B2
Charles Av. DN33	14 D5
Charles Av. DN36	17 G3
Charles Av. DN37	12 A5
Charles Hume Ct. DN32	9 H4
Charles St. DN35	10 D4
Charlton St. DN31	8 C4
Chatsworth Rd. DN35	11 A5
Cheapside. DN37	16 C5
Cheesemans Clo. DN37	16 C5
Cheesemans La. DN37	16 C5
Chelmsford Av. DN34	8 B6
Chelmsford Pl. DN34	8 B6
Chelsea Wk. DN35	11 E8
Chepstow Gro. DN34	14 A2
Cherry Dale. DN35	11 B6
Cherry Tree Cres. DN34	7 H6
Cheshire Wk. DN37	7 G4
Chester Grange. DN33	15 E5
Chester Pl. DN35	11 A5
Chester Wk. DN34	14 A2
Chestnut Av. DN31	8 C5
Chestnut Clo. DN37	16 A6
Chestnut Rd. DN37	16 A5
Chestnut Wk. DN37	6 D3
Chichester Rd. DN35	11 D6
Chiltern Dri. DN37	16 B6
Chiltern Way. DN33	16 D1
Chingford Av. DN34	14 A2
Chippendale Clo. DN36	18 D2
Christine Pl. DN33	17 E1
Church Av. DN36	18 D2
Church Clo. DN32	15 H1
Church La, Bradley. DN37	13 G4
Church La, Grimsby. DN31	4 B4
Church La, Holton le Clay. DN36	19 F5
Church La, Humberston. DN36	19 E3
Church La, Laceby. DN37	12 B5
Church La, Scartho. DN33	14 D5
Church La, Waltham. DN37	16 C5
Church La, Weelsby. DN32	15 H1
Church St. DN32	9 F3
Church Vw. DN34	7 G6
Church Vw. DN37	16 C5
Church Wk. DN35	19 F5
Churchill Way. DN32	4 F3
Clare Ct. DN34	14 A1
Claremont Rd. DN32	10 B4
Clarendon Rd. DN34	13 G3
Clark Av. DN31	8 B5
Clavering St. DN31	8 B3
Clay La. DN36	19 F4
Claymore Clo. DN35	10 C4
Clayton Wk. DN31	4 B3
Clee Cres. DN32	10 A4
Clee Fields Clo. DN32	15 H2
Clee Rd. DN32	10 A4
Clee Village. DN32	10 A4
Cleeness Dri. DN31	19 E1
Cleethorpes Chalet Pk. DN36	19 H2

Cleethorpe Rd. DN31	9 E3	Deene Clo. DN34	13 F3	Evelyn Gro Sth. DN32	9 H6	Glebe Rd. DN35	10 D4
Clerke St. DN35	9 H4	Defender Dri. DN37	7 E5	Evendine Ct. DN36	19 G6	Glebe Rd. DN36	18 D3
Cleveland St. DN31	8 B3	Delamere Ct. DN35	11 D8	Evesham Av. DN34	13 G2	Gleneagles. DN37	16 A5
Clifton Rd. DN34	8 B6	Denby Dri. DN35	11 A6	Exeter Ct. DN34	13 F3	Glenfield Rd. DN37	7 F4
Clixby Clo. DN35	11 E6	Dene Rd. DN32	15 E2			Gloria Way. DN37	7 E5
Clumber Pl. DN35	11 C5	Derry Way. DN33	16 C1	Fair View Av. DN35	10 C4	Gloucester Av. DN34	14 B2
Colin Av. DN32	9 H6	Derwent Dri. DN36	18 C1	Fairfax Rd. DN34	8 B5	Goldgarth. DN32	15 G2
College Av. DN33	16 D1	Devonshire Av. DN32	14 D2	Fairfield Av. DN33	16 C2	Goring Pl. DN35	10 B3
College Gdns. DN33	16 D1	Dial Sq. DN31	4 C3	Fairfield Ct. DN35	11 E8	Gorton St. DN31	9 F2
College St. DN34	8 C6	Digby Gdns. DN34	14 A2	Fairfield Rd. DN35	16 C2	Gosport Rd. DN34	8 A6
College St. DN35	10 C3	Dixon Av. DN32	15 E2	Fairmont Rd. DN32	9 G6	Grafton St. DN32	9 G3
Collingwood Cres. DN34	13 F3	Dolby Vale. DN33	14 A3	Fairway. DN37	16 C5	Grainsby Av. DN35	11 B6
Colson Pl. DN35	9 H5	Dolphin St. DN35	10 D3	Fairway Ct. DN35	19 F1	Grainsby Av. DN36	19 G6
Coltsfoot Dri. DN37	16 A5	Dominion Ct. DN36	17 G3	Fallowfield Rd. DN35	16 B2	Grampian Way. DN33	16 C1
Columbia Rd. DN32	9 G6	Donnington St. DN32	4 F4	Farebrother St. DN32	15 E1	Grange Av. DN37	12 B5
Columbus Way. DN33	13 H4	Dorothy Av. DN37	16 C4	Faringdon Rd. DN31	9 G2	Grange Wk. DN34	8 A6
Combe St. DN35	10 A2	Doughty Clo. DN37	16 C4	Fauconberg Av. DN33	14 C5	Grant St, Cleethorpes. DN35	10 C3
Comber Pl. DN32	9 F4	Doughty Rd. DN32	4 C3	Faulding Way. DN37	7 E5	Grant St, Grimsby. DN35	9 H3
Compton Dri. DN34	8 C6	Douglas Av. DN31	8 B5	Felstead Rd. DN34	7 H6	Grantham Av. DN33	14 D5
Coningsby Dri. DN34	14 B2	Douglas St. DN35	10 B2	Fenby Clo. DN37	7 F6	Granville St. DN32	15 F1
Coniston Av. DN33	16 B2	Dovedale. DN31	16 D2	Fenwick Ct. DN36	19 F6	Grasby Cres. DN37	7 F5
Coniston Cres. DN36	18 C2	Dover St. DN31	4 A2	Ferndale Way. DN31	4 B1	Grasmere Gro. DN36	18 C2
Connaught Av. DN32	14 D2	Downing Clo. DN34	13 H1	Ferndown. DN37	7 G3	Grayling Clo. DN37	7 G5
Connisborough Av. DN36	17 F3	Drake Av. DN32	15 H1	Fernhill. DN37	7 F6	Great Coates Rd,	
Convamore Rd. DN32	4 F3	Drew Av. DN32	15 F3	Fernie St. DN35	11 C7	Gt Coates. DN37	7 E4
Conway Av. DN34	8 A5	Drury Clo. DN37	16 A5	Ferriby La. DN33	14 C5	Great Coates Rd,	
Conyard Rd. DN35	10 C3	Drury La. DN36	17 G3	Field Clo. DN37	12 B5	Healing. DN37	6 B3
Conyers Av. DN33	14 D5	Duchess St. DN32	4 B4	Fieldhouse Rd. DN36	19 E1	Great Grimsby Business Pk.	
Cooks La. DN37	7 F3	Dudley Pl. DN35	11 B5	Fields St. DN31	4 B2	DN37	7 G2
Cooper La. DN37	12 A4	Dudley St. DN31	8 C5	Filey Rd. DN32	15 G2	Green Hill. DN35	11 B6
Cooper Rd. DN32	9 G6	Dugard Rd. DN35	9 H5	Fillingham Cres. DN35	11 D6	Greenfinch Dri. DN35	11 C8
Coppergate. DN37	12 A6	Duke St. DN32	9 G4	Findlay Cres. DN37	17 H3	Greenlands Av. DN36	17 G3
Coral Dri. DN37	16 B4	Dunbar Av. DN36	17 F3	Fircroft Way. DN34	8 B5	Greenway. DN37	16 D6
Corinthian Av. DN34	8 B6	Duncombe Gdns. DN32	4 E1	Firsby Cres. DN33	14 A4	Greethams La. DN32	10 A4
Cormorant Dri. DN37	7 E5	Duncombe St. DN32	4 E1	First Av. DN33	14 C2	Grey Friars. DN37	7 F5
Cornwell Clo. DN33	14 C3	Dunmow St. DN31	8 C4	Fish Dock Rd. DN31	9 F3	Grime St. DN31	4 D2
Coronation Rd. DN35	10 D4	Durban Rd. DN32	9 G5	Fisher Pl. DN35	10 B3	Grimsby Rd,	
Corporation Rd. DN31	4 A1	Durham Av. DN34	8 A5	Fishermans Wharf. DN31	4 B2	Cleethorpes. DN35	10 A1
Cosgrove St. DN35	10 D3	Durham Rd. DN35	11 A5	Fitzwilliam Mews. DN35	11 C7	Grimsby Rd,	
Cotswold Dri. DN37	16 B6	Dursley Av. DN36	17 F3	Fleetwood Clo. DN33	16 C2	Humberston. DN36	11 B7
Cottage Yard La. DN36	18 D4	Dymoke Dri. DN37	7 F6	Fletcher Rd. DN34	7 H6	Grimsby Rd, Laceby. DN37	12 B5
Cottages Plot. DN37	13 F3			Fletchers Yd. DN32	4 B4	Grimsby Rd, Waltham. DN37	16 D4
Cottesmore Rd. DN35	11 C7	Earl Av. DN36	17 H2	Florence St. DN32	15 E1	Grosvenor Ct. DN35	11 E8
Coulam Pl. DN36	19 E2	Earl St. DN31	4 A3	Flottergate Mall. DN31	4 B3	Grosvenor Cres. DN32	4 A4
Coulbeck Dri. DN35	11 B5	East End Clo. DN33	15 E5	Flour Sq. DN31	9 E3	Grosvenor St. DN32	4 A4
Coventry Av. DN34	14 A1	East Gate. DN32	4 D2	Fords Av. DN37	6 C3	Grove Cres. DN32	10 A3
Coxhill Gdns. DN34	13 H2	East Marsh St. DN31	4 D2	Forest Dri. DN36	19 F2	Grove La. DN37	16 C6
Cragston Av. DN33	14 D4	East St Marys Gate. DN31	4 B3	Forest Way. DN36	19 F2	Guildford St. DN32	9 G4
Craithie Rd. DN35	11 C5	East St. DN31	4 D3	Forge Way. DN37	19 F4	Gunby Pl. DN35	11 C5
Crake Av. DN33	14 C5	Eastbourne Way. DN33	16 D2	Forsythia Rise. DN33	14 C5	Gunners Way. DN34	13 F2
Crampin Rd. DN35	10 C3	Eastern Inway. DN34	14 A2	Fortuna Way. DN37	7 E5		
Cranbourne Clo. DN35	11 D8	Eastfield. DN36	19 E2	Fotherby St. DN31	4 D1	Haigh St. DN35	10 E4
Cranwell Dri. DN37	7 H4	Eastfield Av. DN35	17 E2	Fountain Clo. DN37	16 B4	Haile Rd. DN36	19 E1
Craven Rd. DN35	9 H5	Eastfield Rise. DN36	19 F5	Fountains Av. DN37	7 G4	Hainton Av. DN32	4 E4
Crescent St. DN31	4 A3	Eastside Rd. DN31	9 F3	Foxhill. DN37	7 F6	Hallcroft St. DN35	8 C5
Cressy St. DN31	9 E3	Eastville Rd. DN33	14 A4	Frankland Pl. DN35	10 B2	Halton Pl. DN35	11 B6
Cridling Pl. DN35	11 B5	Eastwood Av. DN34	14 D2	Fraser St. DN32	4 F3	Halton Way. DN34	14 B2
Cromer Av. DN34	14 A2	Eaton Ct. DN34	14 C1	Frederick St. DN31	4 A1	Hamilton Clo. DN34	13 F2
Cromwell Rd. DN31	8 A4	Edge Av. DN33	14 D4	Frederick St. DN35	10 C3	Hamilton St. DN32	9 G3
Cromwell Rd. DN35	11 E5	Edinburgh Dri. DN36	19 E4	Frederick Ward Way. DN31	4 A2	Hamont Rd. DN32	10 A3
Cromwell Rd. DN37	7 G3	Edmonds Way. DN31	4 B2	Freeman St. DN36	19 G5	Hampton Ct. DN35	11 B5
Crosby Rd. DN33	14 A4	Edward St. DN32	4 E4	Freeman St. DN32	4 E2	Hardys Rd. DN35	11 D5
Crosland Rd. DN37	7 F4	Edward St. DN35	10 C4	Freeston St. DN35	9 H5	Hare St. DN32	9 F6
Cross Coates Rd. DN34	8 B6	Egton Way. DN37	7 G4	Freshney Dri. DN31	4 A1	Hargrave St. DN32	8 C4
*Cross La, Pinfold La. DN33	14 D6	Elderberry Way. DN35	11 B7	Friargate. DN31	4 B3	Harlech Way. DN32	4 E1
Cross St. DN31	9 F2	Eleanor St. DN32	4 E2	Friargate Sq. DN31	4 B3	Harlestone Ct. DN34	13 F2
Cross St. DN35	10 C3	Elizabeth Clo. DN35	16 C2	Friary Wk. DN31	4 B3	Harlow St. DN31	8 B3
Cross St. DN37	16 C5	Ellesmere Dri. DN34	13 F3	Frobisher Av. DN32	15 H1	Harneis Cres. DN37	12 B4
Crow Hill Av. DN35	10 C4	Ellis Way. DN31	4 D2	Frusher Av. DN33	14 D3	Harold St. DN32	9 G4
Crowland Av. DN34	13 H2	Elliston St. DN35	10 A2	Fuller St. DN35	10 B2	Harrington St. DN35	10 A1
Crowle Dri. DN33	14 A4	Elm Av. DN34	8 A6	Fulstow Gro. DN33	14 B4	Harrison St. DN31	8 C5
Croxby Av. DN33	16 D1	Elm Av. DN35	10 C4			Hart St. DN35	10 A2
Croxby Gro. DN32	16 D2	Elm Gro. DN37	6 C3	Garbutt Pl. DN35	11 E6	Harvest Cres. DN37	16 A5
Cumberland Av. DN32	14 D2	Elm Rd. DN35	10 C4	Garden Dri. DN36	17 G2	Hatton Gro. DN33	14 B4
Cumberland Rd. DN35	11 E8	Elm Rd. DN37	16 C6	Garden St. DN32	4 B4	Haven Av. DN31	8 C4
Curry Rd. DN34	7 H6	Elsenham Rd. DN31	8 B3	Garibaldi St. DN32	4 E1	Haven Ter. DN31	4 A2
Curzon Av. DN35	11 B5	Elsham Dri. DN37	16 B6	Garner St. DN32	15 E1	Haven Wk. DN31	4 C3
Curzon Ct. DN35	11 B5	Elsham Gro. DN33	14 B3	Garnett St. DN35	10 B2	Haverstoe Pl. DN35	11 A6
Cuttleby. DN35	10 D4	Elwyn Pl. DN35	11 B7	Garth La. DN31	4 B2	Hawerby Rd. DN37	12 A4
Cynthia Rd. DN32	10 A4	Emfield Gro. DN33	16 C3	Garthway. DN36	19 F6	Hawkins Gro. DN32	15 H1
Cyrano Way. DN37	7 E5	Emfield Rd. DN33	16 B2	Garton Gro. DN32	15 G2	Hawthorne Av. DN33	16 D1
*Cyril Cooper Ct,		Enfield Av. DN36	17 H3	Gate La. DN33	14 D6	Hawthorne Av. DN35	10 B2
Abbey Dri East. DN32	8 D6	Ennerdale Clo. DN36	18 C2	Gate Way. DN31	8 C2	Hawthorne Av. DN37	17 F4
		Enterprise Way. DN32	9 G6	Gayton St. DN35	11 E6	Haycroft Av. DN31	8 C5
Daggett Rd. DN35	11 E6	Escart Rd. DN32	9 H6	Gedney Clo. DN37	7 F5	Hayling Mere. DN35	11 D8
Dale Vw. DN31	4 A4	Eskdale Way. DN37	7 F4	George Janney Ct. DN32	9 F4	Hays Clo. DN36	19 F5
Dame Kendal Gro. DN33	14 C3	Eskham Clo. DN35	11 D6	George St. DN35	10 D4	Heathfield Ct. DN34	14 C1
Danesfield Av. DN37	16 C4	Estate Rd No. 1. DN31	7 H2	Georges St. DN31	4 C3	Helene Gro. DN32	10 A3
Daubney St. DN35	10 A2	Estate Rd No. 2. DN31	7 H3	Gertrude St. DN32	15 E2	Hemswell Dri. DN37	7 H4
Davenport Dri. DN35	11 A5	Estate Rd No. 3. DN31	7 H2	Gibraltar La. DN37	12 A4	Heneage Rd. DN32	4 E3
David Pl. DN36	17 G4	Estate Rd No. 4. DN31	7 H2	Gilbey Rd. DN31	8 B3	Henry St. DN31	8 C4
David St. DN32	15 F1	Estate Rd No. 5. DN31	7 H2	Giles St. DN35	10 C4	Hereford Av. DN34	14 C2
Davie Pl. DN35	9 H5	Estate Rd No. 6. DN31	7 H2	Glebe Clo,		Heritage Sq. DN31	4 C2
Davisons Av. DN35	4 B1	Estate Rd No. 7. DN31	7 H3	Holton le Clay. DN36	19 F4	Heron Clo. DN32	15 H2
Dawlish Rd. DN33	16 D3	Estuary Way. DN31	8 B2	Glebe Clo,		Heron Way. DN36	19 F4
Deangate. DN31	4 A4	Europa Business Pk. DN31	8 B2	Humberston. DN36	18 D4	Hewitts Av. DN36	11 A8
Deaton La. DN36	17 G3	Evelyn Gro Nth. DN32	9 H6	Glebe Rd. DN33	15 E5	Hewitts Manor. DN35	11 B7

Hewson Rd. DN36 19 E2
Hey St. DN35 11 D5
Heythorp Rd. DN35 11 C7
High St, Cleethorpes. DN35 10 D3
High St, Laceby. DN37 12 B5
High St, Waltham. DN37 16 C5
High Thorpe Cres. DN35 11 B6
Highcliff Rd. DN35 10 E4
Highfield Av. DN32 15 E1
Highgate. DN35 10 D4
Hilary Rd. DN33 16 D2
Hilary Way. DN37 7 G4
Hilton Ct. DN35 19 F1
Hinkler St. DN35 10 D4
Holles St. DN32 4 E2
Hollingsworth Clo. DN35 11 B7
Holme Av. DN36 17 G3
Holme Farm Clo. DN37 7 G3
Holme St. DN32 4 D3
Holton Cl. DN36 19 F6
Holton Mt. DN36 19 F5
Holyoake Av. DN32 10 A4
Home Paddock. DN37 16 C5
Homefield Av. DN33 14 D3
Hope St. DN32 9 G3
Hope St. DN35 10 E4
Howard Gro. DN32 15 H1
Howlett Rd. DN35 11 E5
Huddleston Rd. DN32 9 G6
Humber Bank Sth. DN31 9 G2
Humber Bridge. DN31 9 G3
Humber Bridge Rd. DN31 9 G3
Humber St. DN31 9 G3
Humber St. DN35 10 D4
Humber Ter. DN31 4 A2
Humberston Av. DN36 18 A4
Humberston Rd. DN36 18 D2
Humberston Rd. DN35 11 A5
Humberstone Rd. DN32 9 G5
Hume St. DN31 8 C5
Hunsley Cres. DN32 15 H3
Hunters Clo. DN37 7 E4
Hurford Pl. DN33 16 C3
Hurstlea Dri. DN36 19 E1
Hutchinson Rd. DN35 10 C2
Hutton Rd. DN31 9 F2

Imperial Av. DN35 10 A2
INDUSTRIAL ESTATES:
Acorn Business Centre. DN31 4 C4
Alexandra Retail Pk. DN31 4 C1
Birchin Way Ind Est. DN31 8 B3
Europa Business Pk. DN31 8 B2
Great Grimsby Business Pk. DN37 7 G2
South Humberside Ind Est. DN31 7 H3
West Marsh Ind Est. DN32 4 B1
Ingleby Gro. DN37 7 H5
Ingram Pl. DN35 11 B7
Ings La. DN37 16 C5
Intax Farm Mews. DN32 15 F1
Iona Dri. DN36 19 F2
Irby Ct. DN35 11 B6
Isaacs Hill. DN35 10 C3
Itterby Cres. DN35 11 A6

Jackson St. DN31 4 A1
Jacksons Pl. DN36 18 B1
James St. DN31 8 C4
Janton Ct. DN36 17 G2
Jenner Pl. DN35 9 H5
Johnson St. DN35 9 H4
Joseph St. DN31 8 C4
Julian St. DN32 9 F5
Juniper Way. DN33 14 C5
Jutland Ct. DN36 17 H2

Kathleen Av. DN35 10 B2
Kathleen Gro. DN32 10 A3
Kaymile Clo. DN36 17 G3
Keir Hardie Wk. DN32 4 C4
Keith Cres. DN37 12 A5
Kelham Rd. DN32 10 B4
Kelstern Rd. DN34 14 A2
Kemeshame Ct. DN37 16 D5
Kemp Rd. DN31 9 G1
Kenford Ct. DN36 17 G3
Kenilworth Rd. BN5 11 B5
Kenmar Rd. DN37 12 A5
Kensington Pl. DN33 17 E1
Kent St. DN32 9 F3
Keston Ct. DN35 11 E6

Kettlewell St. DN32 15 E1
Kew Rd. DN35 10 C4
Kiddier Av. DN33 16 C2
King Edward St. DN31 9 E4
Kings Cl. DN34 14 A1
Kings Mews. DN35 19 F1
Kings Par. DN35 10 E4
Kings Rd, Cleethorpes. DN35 11 E5
Kings Rd, Humberston. DN35 19 F1
Kingsley Gro. DN33 14 C3
Kingston Av. DN34 8 B6
Kingston Clo. DN35 11 E8
Kingsway. DN35 10 E4
Kirk Gate. DN37 16 C5
Kirk Side. DN37 16 C5
Kirkstead Cres. DN33 14 B4
Kirmington Gdns. DN34 8 A6
Knight St. DN32 9 H6
Knights Clo. DN37 12 B5
Knightsbridge. DN36 17 G3
Knoll St. DN35 10 D4
Konigswinter Ct. DN36 17 G3
Kymer Pl. DN35 11 E5

Laburnum Av. DN37 16 B5
Laburnum Clo. DN37 16 B5
Laburnum Dri. DN34 7 G6
Laceby Rd. DN34 13 F3
Lady Frances Cres. DN35 10 A4
Ladysmith Rd. DN32 4 F3
Ladysmith St. DN32 9 F5
Laforey Rd. DN37 7 G2
Lambert Rd. DN32 14 D1
Lampton Gro. DN32 15 E1
Lancaster Av. DN31 8 C5
Lancaster Gate. DN31 19 F6
Lancing Way. DN33 16 C1
Landeck Av. DN34 8 B6
Langdale Av. DN33 16 B2
Langley Pl. DN35 11 E6
Langton Clo. DN33 14 B4
Langton Dri. DN33 14 B3
Langton Rd. DN36 19 G6
Lansdown Link. DN35 11 C6
Lansdowne Av. DN32 14 D3
Larch Av. DN35 11 B7
Larden Av. DN33 16 C2
Larmour Rd. DN37 7 F4
Laurel Clo. DN33 14 C4
Lavenham Rd. DN33 16 B1
Lawrence St. DN31 8 C4
Lawson Av. DN31 8 C5
Leas Clo. DN37 16 C4
Ledbury Rd. DN36 17 H2
Legsby Av. DN32 15 E1
Legsby Pl. DN32 15 E2
Leighton Gro. DN33 14 C3
Lestrange St. DN35 10 A3
Lewis Rd. DN35 10 B2
Lichfield Rd. DN32 9 H6
Lidgard Rd. DN36 19 E2
Limber Ct. DN34 8 A6
Limber Vale. DN34 8 A6
Lime Gro. DN36 19 F6
Lime St. DN31 8 C5
Limetree Av. DN33 14 D4
Lincoln Av. DN31 8 C5
Lincoln Rd. DN35 11 A5
Lindisfarne Av. DN36 17 F3
Lindrick Wk. DN37 16 A5
Lindsey Dri. DN36 19 E4
Lindsey Dri. DN37 6 C3
Lindsey Rise. DN33 16 D1
Lindsey Rd. DN35 11 D5
Lindum Rd. DN35 11 D5
Links Rd. DN35 11 E6
Linwood Av. DN33 16 D1
Lisburn Gro. DN33 14 D4
Lister St. DN31 8 C4
Little Coates Rd. DN34 13 G3
Little Michael St. DN31 8 C5
Littlebeck Rd. DN36 18 C2
Littlefield La. DN34 8 B6
Lock Hill. DN31 9 E3
Loft Av. DN37 7 H4
Lombard St. DN34 8 B5
Lomond Gro. DN36 18 C2
Longfield Rd. DN34 13 G2
Longhorn Clo. DN37 16 A5
Longmeadows Dri. DN37 12 B4
Lonsdale Gro. DN36 18 D4
Lopham La. DN37 12 A6
Lord St. DN31 8 C4
Louth Rd,
  Holton le Clay. DN36 19 E4
Louth Rd,
  New Waltham. DN36 17 F4

Louth Rd, Scartho. DN33 16 D1
Loveden Ct. DN35 11 E6
Lovett St. DN35 10 A2
Low Rd. DN37 6 B3
Lower Burgess St. DN31 4 D1
Lower Spring St. DN31 9 E3
Ludborough Way. DN35 11 D6
Ludford St. DN32 9 E6
Ludgate Clo. DN37 16 C5
Ludlow Av. DN34 8 A5
Ludlow Pl. DN35 11 C5
Lyndhurst Av. DN33 14 D4
Lynton Rise. DN35 11 C6
Lytham Dri. DN37 16 B6

Macaulay St. DN31 8 C5
Maclure St. DN31 9 F2
McVeigh Ct. DN37 6 C3
Magdalene Rd. DN34 14 A1
Magnolia Dri. DN36 19 G6
Maidwell Way. DN34 13 E2
Malcolm Rd. DN34 13 H3
Mallard Clo. DN37 6 B3
Mallard Mews. DN32 9 E6
Malmesbury Dri. DN34 8 C6
Maltby Av. DN37 13 E3
Malvern Av. DN33 14 A3
Manchester St. DN35 10 B2
Mandela Link. DN31 8 C5
Manley Gdns. DN35 11 E6
Manningtree Clo. DN32 9 E6
Manor Av. DN32 4 B4
Manor Ct. DN32 4 B4
Manor Dri. DN37 16 C4
Mansel St. DN32 9 H4
Manson Clo. DN34 13 F3
Maple Av. DN34 7 G6
Maple Gro. DN36 17 F4
Maple Gro. DN37 6 C3
Marcus St. DN34 8 A6
Margaret Pl. DN36 17 G3
Margaret St. DN32 4 E4
Marian Way. DN37 16 A5
Marigold Wk. DN35 11 C8
Market Sq. DN31 4 B3
Market St. DN31 4 D1
Market St. DN35 10 D3
Markham Mews. DN37 16 D5
Marklew Av. DN34 8 B5
Marlborough Way. DN35 11 D8
Marples Mws. DN35 10 E4
Marquis Av. DN36 17 H2
Marsden Rd. DN31 9 G3
Marsh Chapel Clo. DN35 11 D6
Marshall Av. DN34 8 B6
Marton Gro. DN33 14 A4
Martyn Rd. DN35 10 B3
Mathews St. DN35 10 A2
Matlock Dri. DN37 7 H4
Maxwell Ct. DN34 13 F2
May St. DN35 10 B2
Mayfair Ct. DN35 11 E8
Mayfair Cres. DN37 16 B5
Mayfair Dri East. DN37 7 F5
Mayfair Dri West. DN37 7 F5
Mayside Clo. DN36 19 G5
Meadow Ct. DN34 7 G6
Meadow Dri. DN33 16 B1
Meadow Dri. DN36 6 C2
Meadow Vw. DN35 11 D8
Meadowbank. DN37 7 F4
Medway Pl. DN34 14 A2
Melbourne Av. DN34 14 D4
Melrose Way. DN37 7 G4
Mendip Av. DN33 16 C1
Mersey Way. DN37 7 G4
Middle Ct. DN31 4 D2
Middle Thorpe Rd. DN35 11 B6
Midfield Pl. DN36 18 D3
Midfield Rd. DN36 18 D3
Mill Av. DN31 8 C4
Mill Clo. DN37 16 C6
Mill Garth. DN35 11 B7
Mill Hill Cres. DN35 10 C4
Mill Pl. DN35 10 D3
Mill Rd. DN35 10 C4
Mill Vw. DN37 16 C5
Miller Av. DN32 10 A3
Millfield Av. DN33 14 A4
Millom Way. DN32 4 F1
Milton Rd. DN33 14 B3
Minnow Ct. DN37 7 G5
Minshull Rd. DN35 11 D6
Mirfield Rd. DN32 15 F2
Mollison Av. DN35 10 D4
Montague St. DN35 9 H4
Montgomery Rd. DN35 10 B4

Moody La. DN31 7 H1
Moorland Dri. DN36 17 G2
Mordaunt Av. DN33 16 C2
Morgan Way. DN35 10 C4
Morpeth Wk. DN34 8 A6
Morton Rd. DN34 8 B5
Moss St. DN32 4 C4
Moulton Clo. DN34 13 F2
Mount Pleasant. DN36 19 F6
Mount Pleasant. DN37 16 C4
Muirfield. DN37 16 A5
Mulgrave Clo. DN37 7 H4
Murray St. DN31 9 F3

Nacton St. DN31 9 F3
Nairn Way. DN34 14 C1
Nelson St. DN32 9 F3
Nelson Way. DN34 13 F2
Neptune St. DN35 10 C3
Neville St. DN35 10 B2
Neville Turner Way. DN37 16 B5
New Biggin Wk. DN31 4 B3
New Cartergate. DN31 4 A3
New Chapel La. DN37 12 B5
New Clo. DN33 14 C3
New Haven Ter. DN31 8 B3
New Rd. DN35 10 D4
New Rd, Laceby. DN37 12 C5
New Rd, Waltham. DN37 16 C5
New St. DN31 4 C3
Newbury Av. DN37 7 G3
Newbury Gro. DN34 13 G2
Newbury Ter. DN37 7 G3
Newby Rd. DN31 8 C5
Newlands Pk. DN36 19 F1
Newmarch Cres. DN33 14 D6
Newmarket St. DN32 4 E1
Newsham Dri. DN34 8 A6
Newstead Av. DN36 19 G5
Newstead Rd. DN35 11 C5
Newton Gro. DN33 14 C3
Nicholson Rd. DN37 6 C2
Nicholson St. DN35 11 D5
Norfolk La. DN35 10 C3
Normanby Rd. DN34 8 B5
Normandy Rd. DN35 10 B4
Norsefield Av. DN37 16 C4
North Prom. DN35 10 C2
North Quay. DN31 9 G1
North Sea La. DN36 18 D1
North St. DN35 10 D4
Northumberland Clo. DN34 14 C1
Norwich Av. DN34 14 B2

Oak Av. DN32 15 E3
Oak Rd. DN37 6 C2
Oak Way. DN35 11 B7
Oakwood Dri. DN37 7 E6
Old Chapel La. DN37 12 B5
Old Farm Ct. DN37 16 A5
Old Fleet. DN37 7 E6
Old Market Pl. DN31 4 B3
Old Rd. DN37 7 E4
Oliver Ct. DN31 4 A1
Oliver St. DN35 10 B2
Oole Rd. DN35 10 D4
Orby Gro. DN33 14 A3
Orchard Ct. DN37 16 B5
Orchards Croft. DN33 16 D2
Orion Way. DN34 13 F2
Ormsby Clo. DN35 11 B6
Orwell St. DN31 9 F3
Osborne Dri. DN36 19 G6
Osborne St. DN31 4 C3
Osbourne St. DN35 10 D3
Oslear Cres. DN35 10 C4
Oxcombe Clo. DN33 16 B2
Oxford St. DN32 9 G3
Oxford St. DN35 10 D4

Pagehall Clo. DN33 14 D5
Paignton Ct. DN33 16 D2
Park Av. DN32 15 E2
Park Dri. DN32 14 D1
Park La. DN35 11 D8
Park St. DN35 9 H4
Park Vw. DN35 10 A2
Parker Rd. DN36 19 E2
Parker St. DN35 11 D5
Parris Pl. DN35 10 B3
Pasture St. DN31 4 C3
Patrick St. DN32 15 E1
Paul Cres. DN36 18 D2
Peace Haven. DN37 16 B4
Peaks Av. DN36 17 G2
Peaks Field Av. DN32 15 E1
Peaks La. DN32 15 F2

Street	Ref		Street	Ref		Street	Ref		Street	Ref
Peaks La. DN36	17 H3		Ripon St. DN31	8 C5		Scott Clo. DN37	7 H4		Station Rd, Healing. DN37	6 B3
Pearson Rd. DN35	11 D6		Rivan Av. DN33	16 C2		Scrivelsby St. DN35	11 E7		Station Rd,	
Pelham Av. DN33	14 C5		Rivan Gro. DN33	16 C2		Sea Rd. DN35	10 D3		New Waltham. DN36	17 F3
Pelham Pl. DN33	14 C5		Riverside Dri. DN35	19 F1		Sea View St. DN35	10 D4		Station Rd, Waltham. DN37	16 D4
Pelham Rd. DN34	8 C6		Roberts St. DN32	9 F5		Seacroft Rd. DN35	11 E5		Stephen Cres. DN34	13 G3
Pelham Rd. DN35	10 C3		Robinson La. DN31	9 H3		Seaford Rd. DN35	19 E1		Stephen Cres. DN36	18 D2
Pelham Rd. DN36	19 E5		Robinson St East. DN32	4 D3		Seamer Gro. DN32	15 G1		Sterling Cres. DN37	16 A6
Pelham Sq. DN35	10 C2		Robson Rd. DN35	10 B3		Seaton Gro. DN32	15 G2		Stevenson Pl. DN35	10 B4
Pemberton Dri. DN36	17 F3		Rochester Ct. DN35	11 E8		Second Av. DN33	14 C2		Stirling St. DN31	9 G3
Pembroke Ct. DN34	8 A5		Rockingham Ct. DN34	13 F3		Seed Close La. DN37	12 B5		Stokesley Wk. DN37	7 H4
Pembroke Rd. DN34	14 A1		Romsey Ct. DN34	13 F2		Segmere St. DN35	10 E4		Stortford St. DN31	8 B3
Pendreth Pl. DN35	10 B3		Rookery Av. DN33	14 D3		Selbourne Rd. DN34	13 G3		Stow Clo. DN37	7 F4
Penshurst Rd. DN35	11 B5		Rookery Rd. DN37	6 B3		Selge Way. DN33	14 A4		Strand St. DN32	9 F3
Pepper Corn Wk. DN32	4 C4		Ropery St. DN32	4 F4		Service Rd 1. DN37	7 G4		Strange Wk. DN36	18 D2
Peppercorn Wk. DN36	19 F5		Rosaire Pl. DN33	17 E1		Service Rd 2. DN37	7 G4		Stratford Av. DN33	14 A3
Perkins Clo. DN37	7 H4		Rosalind Av. DN34	8 C5		Service Rd 3. DN37	7 G4		Stratton Ct. DN34	13 E2
Pershore Av. DN34	13 F2		Rosedale. DN37	16 B4		Service Rd 4. DN37	7 G4		Strawberry Hill. DN37	16 A5
Petchell Way. DN32	4 E1		Rosemary Av. DN34	13 H1		Service Rd 5. DN37	7 G4		Strubby Clo. DN35	11 E6
Peterhouse Rd. DN34	13 H1		Rosemary Way. DN35	11 C8		Service Rd 6. DN37	7 H4		Stuart Wortley St. DN31	9 F2
Peterhouse Rd. DN34	14 A1		Roseveare Av. DN34	8 B5		Service Rd 7. DN37	7 H4		Sturton Gro. DN33	14 B3
Phelps Pl. DN32	10 A4		Rosina Gro Nth. DN32	9 H6		Service Rd 8. DN37	7 G4		Suggitts Ct. DN35	10 B2
Phelps St. DN35	10 A1		Rosina Gro Sth. DN32	9 H6		Service Rd 9. DN37	7 G4		Suggitts La. DN35	10 B2
Philip Av. DN35	11 B5		Ross Rd. DN31	9 G3		Service Rd 10. DN37	7 G4		Suggitts Orchard. DN35	10 C2
Philip Av. DN37	16 C4		Rothwell Av. DN33	14 B4		Service Rd 11. DN37	7 G4		Summerfield Av. DN37	16 C4
Philip Gro. DN35	11 B6		Roundway. DN34	14 C2		Service Rd 12. DN37	7 G3		Summerfield Clo. DN37	16 C4
Phillips La. DN37	12 B5		Rowan Dri. DN36	19 E2		Service Rd 13. DN37	7 G3		Sunningdale. DN37	16 A5
Phoenix St. DN32	4 C4		Rowan Dri. DN37	6 B2		Service Rd 15. DN37	7 G4		Sunny Cnr. DN33	14 D5
Phyllis Av. DN34	8 C6		Rowston St. DN35	10 E4		Service Rd 16. DN37	7 G4		Surtees St. DN31	9 F2
Phyllis Taylors Gdns. DN32	4 C4		Royal Ct. DN35	19 F1		Service Rd 17. DN37	7 H4		Sussex St. DN35	9 H4
Piccadilly. DN36	17 G3		Royal St. DN31	9 E3		Service Rd 18. DN37	7 H4		Sutcliffe Av. DN35	14 A3
Picksley Cres. DN36	19 F6		Rudham Av. DN32	15 E3		Service Rd 19. DN37	7 H4		Swaby Dri. DN35	11 B6
Pine Clo. DN37	7 G3		Rufford Rd. DN35	11 C5		Service Rd 20. DN37	7 H5		Swales Rd. DN36	19 E2
Pine Ct. DN35	11 B7		Runswick Rd. DN32	9 G6		Service Rd 21. DN37	7 G4		Swallow Dri. DN37	6 B3
Pine Wk. DN37	6 C3		Russell Ct. DN35	11 E8		Service Rd 22. DN37	7 G4		Sweetbriar Clo. DN37	16 A4
Pinewood Cres. DN33	14 A4		Rutland Ct. DN32	9 G5		Service Rd 23. DN37	7 G4		Swiftsure Cres. DN34	13 F2
Pinfold Gdns. DN36	19 G6		Rutland Dri. DN36	17 G4		Service Rd 26. DN37	7 G4		Swinderby Gdns. DN34	14 A2
Pinfold La. DN33	14 D6		Rutland St. DN32	9 G5		Severn Way. DN37	7 G4		Sycamore Av. DN33	14 D4
Pinfold La. DN36	19 F5		Rydal Av. DN33	16 C2		Shaftesbury Mews. DN36	17 G3		
Poplar La. DN37	19 F1					Shaw Dri. DN33	17 E1		Tallert Way. DN33	13 H4
Poplar Gro. DN35	10 C3		Sackville St. DN34	8 C6		Sheepfold St. DN32	4 D3		Tamar Dri. DN36	17 H2
Poplar Rd. DN35	10 C3		St Andrews Dri. DN32	15 H2		Shelley Av. DN33	14 B3		Tasburgh. DN32	9 F6
Poplar Rd. DN37	6 B2		St Andrews Rd. DN36	19 E2		Sheraton Dri. DN36	18 D2		Tattershall Av. DN34	13 H3
Portland Av. DN32	15 E2		St Anns Av. DN34	8 C6		Sherburn St. DN35	11 C5		Taunton Way. DN34	16 D1
Portland Pl. DN32	15 E2		St Augustine Av. DN32	15 E2		Sherwood Dri. DN34	13 G2		Taylor St. DN35	9 H3
Pretymen Cres. DN36	17 G3		St Chads Gate. DN37	7 G4		Side La. DN37	17 E2		Taylors Av. DN35	11 B7
Princes Rd. DN35	10 C3		St Chads Wk Sth. DN37	7 G4		Sidney Pl. DN33	9 H4		Tealby Gro. DN33	14 B3
Princess Av. DN31	4 A4		St Christophers Rd. DN36	18 D2		Sidney Rd. DN34	8 B5		Team Gate. DN37	7 E6
Priors Clo. DN36	17 H4		St Francis Gro. DN37	12 A5		Sidney St. DN35	9 H4		Telford Pl. DN34	8 A5
Priory Rd. DN37	7 F6		St Giles Avenue. DN33	14 D6		Sidney Taylor Wk. DN36	17 G2		Tenby Wk. DN34	8 B5
Prystie Pl. DN35	11 B7		St Helens Av. DN33	14 D3		Signhills Av. DN35	11 E5		Tennyson Mews. DN31	4 B1
Purbeck Rd. DN33	16 C1		St Heliers Rd. DN35	10 C3		Silver St. DN31	4 B3		Tennyson Rd. DN35	10 C3
Pyewipe Rd. DN31	8 C4		St Hildas Av. DN34	8 C6		Silver St. DN36	19 F6		Tennyson St. DN31	4 B1
Pytchley Wk. DN35	11 C7		St Hughs Av. DN35	10 C4		Silvergarth. DN32	15 G2		Terrington Pl. DN35	11 B5
			St Ives Cres. DN34	13 G2		Simons Pl. DN35	10 B3		Tetney La. DN36	19 G5
Quantock Rd. DN33	16 C1		St James Av. DN34	8 A6		Sinderson Rd. DN36	19 E2		Tetney Rd. DN36	18 D3
Queen Elizabeth Rd. DN36	18 D2		St James Ct. DN34	8 C6		Sixhills St. DN32	4 D3		Tewkesbury Dri. DN34	8 C6
Queen Mary Av. DN35	10 A2		St James Sq. DN31	4 B4		Skinners La. DN37	16 C5		The Avenue,	
Queen St. DN31	4 D3		St Johns Ct. DN34	14 A1		Solomon Ct. DN35	11 B5		Great Coates. DN37	7 F4
Queens Ct. DN34	14 A1		St Johns Rd. DN36	18 D2		Somersby St. DN31	4 B2		The Avenue, Healing. DN37	6 B3
Queens Par. DN31	4 A3		St Lukes Cres. DN36	18 D2		Sophia Av. DN33	14 C6		The Berea. DN34	14 C2
Queens Par. DN35	11 D5		St Lukes St. DN32	4 F2		South Humberside Ind Est.			The Cloisters. DN36	19 E3
Queensway. DN37	7 G4		St Margarets Clo. DN37	12 A5		DN31	7 H3		The Cloisters. DN37	7 F6
Quorn Mews. DN35	11 C7		St Marks Rd. DN36	18 D2		South Parade. DN31	4 B2		The Close. DN34	8 C6
Quinton Rd. DN32	15 E2		St Martins Cres. DN33	14 D3		South Sea La. DN36	18 D4		The Copse. DN33	16 D1
			St Marys Gate. DN32	10 A4		South St Marys Gate. DN31	4 B3		The Crescent. DN35	19 E5
Radcliffe Rd. DN37	6 C3		St Mathews Rd. DN36	18 D2		South St. DN35	10 E4		The Crest. DN34	14 C2
Railway Pl. DN31	9 F3		St Mawes Cres. DN34	8 A5		South Vw. DN34	8 A6		The Crofts. DN36	18 D2
Railway St. DN32	4 E1		St Michaels Rd. DN34	13 G2		South Vw,			The Crossway. DN34	13 G3
Railway Ter. DN32	4 C4		St Nicholas Dri. DN37	7 E6		Holton le Clay. DN36	19 G6		The Drawing Ct. DN33	8 B2
Raithby Gro. DN33	14 A4		St Olafs Gro. DN32	9 E6		South Vw,			The Elms. DN36	18 D3
Ravendale Clo. DN36	19 G6		St Peters Av. DN35	10 C3		Humberston. DN36	18 D2		The Lanes. DN34	8 C6
Ravendale Rd. DN35	11 E6		St Peters Clo. DN36	19 F5		Southern Wk. DN33	16 D2		The Mead. DN37	12 B5
Ravenhill Clo. DN35	11 B6		St Peters Cres. DN36	18 D2		Southfield Av. DN33	16 D2		The Orchard. DN36	17 G3
Ravensburn St. DN31	4 A1		St Peters Gro. DN37	12 A5		Southfield Clo. DN33	16 D2		The Oval. DN33	14 C5
Ravensburn Way. DN31	4 A2		St Thomas Clo. DN36	18 D3		Southfield Rd. DN36	19 F6		The Ridgeway. DN33	13 F3
Ravenscar Rd. DN37	7 G4		Salamander Clo. DN31	8 C4		Southland Way. DN37	7 H4		The Smooting. DN36	19 F5
Recto Av. DN32	15 F2		Salisbury Av. DN34	8 B6		Southwold Cres. DN33	16 C1		The Spinney. DN34	8 C6
Redbourne Rd. DN33	14 B4		Salisbury Av. DN37	16 B5		Sovereign Clo. DN34	13 F3		The Square. DN32	9 G4
Redcar Gro. DN32	15 G2		Salisbury Dri. DN37	16 B5		Spark St. DN34	8 B5		Thesiger St. DN32	9 F4
Redwood Dri. DN35	11 B7		Salmeston St. DN34	8 C6		Spencer St. DN31	9 H3		Thirkleby Cres. DN32	15 G2
Regent Gdns. DN34	14 D1		Saltburn Gro. DN32	15 G2		Spring Bank. DN34	8 A5		Thirlmere Av. DN33	16 C2
Remillo Av. DN32	15 F2		Saltgate. DN37	7 G4		Spring La. DN37	12 B5		Thomas St. DN32	4 F3
Rendel St. DN31	8 D4		Salvesen Rd. DN31	9 H3		Springfield Rd. DN33	16 B1		Thoresby Pl. DN35	11 C6
Reporto Av. DN32	15 F2		Samuel Av. DN32	9 H6		Springway Cres. DN34	8 A5		Thoresway Gro. DN35	14 A4
Responso Av. DN32	15 F2		Sanctuary Way. DN37	7 E6		Springwood Cres. DN33	16 B2		Thorganby Rd. DN35	11 E6
Reston Gro. DN33	14 B3		Sanders St. DN31	8 C5		Spurn Av. DN33	16 D1		Thornhill Gdns. DN35	8 A5
Revesby Av. DN34	13 H3		Sandford St. DN31	8 C4		Stainton Av. DN33	14 A3		Thornton Clo. DN36	17 G2
Revigo Av. DN32	15 F2		Sandringham Rd. DN35	11 B5		Stallingborough Rd. DN37	6 A5		Thornton Cres. DN36	11 C5
Reynolds St. DN35	10 B3		Sargon Way. DN37	7 H2		Stanford Clo. DN37	12 B4		Thornton Gro. DN34	13 G3
Rialto Av. DN32	15 F2		Saunby Gro. DN35	10 C3		Stanhope Pl. DN35	10 A3		Thorold St. DN31	9 G3
Riby Ct. DN36	19 G5		Savoy Ct. DN31	4 C3		Stanland Way. DN36	18 D2		Thrunscoe Rd. DN35	11 D5
Riby Sq. DN31	9 F3		Saxby Gro. DN33	14 A3		Stanley St. DN32	9 G5		Timberley Dri. DN37	7 F5
Riby St. DN31	9 F3		Saxon Cres. DN34	10 C4		Station Av. DN36	17 G3		Tintern Wk. DN37	7 G3
Richard St. DN31	8 C4		Scampton Clo. DN34	14 B2		Station Rd,			Tiverton Wk. DN35	10 A2
Richardson Clo. DN36	19 E3		Scartho Rd. DN33	14 D3		Cleethorpes. DN35	10 D3		Toll Bar Av. DN36	17 F3
Richmond Ct. DN34	8 B6		Scawby Rd. DN33	14 A4		Station Rd,			Tom Hammond Way. DN32	9 F4
Richmond Rd. DN35	11 C5		School Wk. DN35	11 A5		Great Coates. DN37	7 F4		Tomline St. DN31	9 F3

23

Tonbridge Wk. DN33	16 C1	Wellgarth. DN32	15 G2
Tonnant Way. DN34	13 F2	Wellington St. DN32	4 E2
Toothill Gdns. DN34	7 H6	Wellowgate DN32	4 B4
Toothill Rd. DN34	7 H6	Wellowgate Mews. DN32	4 B4
Torbay Dri. DN33	16 C3	Wells Cres. DN35	11 C7
Torksey Dri. DN33	14 B3	Wells Rd. DN37	6 A3
Torrington St. DN32	15 F1	Wells St. DN31	8 C5
Totnes Rd. DN33	16 C3	Wendover Clo. DN36	19 E3
Town Hall Sq. DN31	4 C3	Wendover Rise. DN35	11 D5
Town Hall St. DN31	4 C3	Wentworth Rd. DN34	8 B5
Townsend Clo. DN36	19 F1	Werneth Rd. DN32	4 E2
Toynton Pl. DN33	14 B4	Wesley Cres. DN35	11 C6
Toynton Rd. DN33	14 B3	West Coates Rd. DN31	8 C3
*Toynton Wk,		West Lea. DN33	16 D2
Toynton Rd. DN33	14 B4	West Marsh Ind Est. DN32	4 B1
Trafalgar Av. DN34	13 F2	West St Marys Gate. DN31	4 B3
Trafalgar Pl. DN36	17 H2	West St. DN35	10 D4
Tranby Dri. DN37	15 H2	Westbourne Gro. DN33	16 D2
Trevor Clo. DN37	12 B5	Westbury Pk. DN35	11 E8
Trinity Rd. DN35	11 C5	Westcroft Rd. DN35	11 E8
Trinity St. DN31	9 G3	Westerdale Way. DN37	7 G4
Tunnard St. DN32	9 G4	Western Outway. DN34	14 A2
Turnberry App. DN37	16 B5	Westfield Av. DN33	14 D3
Twyning Pl. DN35	10 B2	Westfield Gro. DN35	10 B4
Tyler Av. DN31	8 B5	Westfield Rd. DN37	16 B5
Tyne Way. DN37	7 G4	Westgate. DN31	8 D3
		Westhill Rd. DN34	14 B1
Ulster Av. DN34	14 D4	Westkirke Av. DN33	17 E1
Unity Rd. DN32	10 A4	Westlands Av. DN34	14 C1
Upper Burgess St. DN31	4 D2	Westminster Dri. DN34	8 C6
Upper Burgess St. DN31	4 D3	Westport Rd. DN35	11 E8
Upper Spring St. DN31	4 D2	Westside Rd. DN31	8 C2
Utterby Dri. DN34	14 C1	Westward Clo. DN34	14 C2
		Westward Ho. DN34	14 B1
Vaughan Av. DN32	15 H2	Westwood Rd. DN37	6 B2
Veal St. DN31	8 C5	Weyford Rd. DN35	11 E8
Vicarage Gdns. DN34	8 C6	Wharfedale Way. DN31	4 B1
Vicarage Lawn. DN34	8 C6	Wharncliffe Rd Nth. DN31	9 F1
Victor St. DN32	9 G3	Wharton St. DN31	8 C5
Victoria Ct. DN31	4 C1	Wheatfield Dri. DN37	16 A5
Victoria Rd. DN31	4 C1	Whernside Wk. DN31	4 B2
Victoria St Sth. DN31	4 C1	Whimbrel Way. DN36	17 H2
Victoria St West. DN31	4 B3	Whisby Clo. DN34	19 G5
Victory Way. DN34	13 F3	Whitehall Country Cotts.	
Viscount Way. DN36	19 F2	DN35	11 E8
Vivian Av. DN32	15 H2	Whitehall Rd. DN35	11 E8
		Whites Rd. DN35	11 D5
Waby Clo. DN37	7 F4	Whitgift Clo. DN37	12 B5
Waddingham Pl. DN36	17 H4	Whitgift Way. DN37	7 G4
Waddington Pl. DN34	14 A2	Wickham Rd. DN31	9 G3
Waldorf Rd. DN35	11 E8	Wicklow Av. DN33	16 C1
WalesbyClo. DN33	16 B2	William St. DN35	10 D4
Walk La. DN36	18 D4	Willing Way. DN32	4 F2
Walker Av. DN33	16 D1	Willingham St. DN32	4 D4
Wall St. DN34	8 B5	Willoughby Gro. DN34	13 H2
Walmsgate. DN33	14 B3	Wilson St. DN35	10 B2
Walmsgate Pl. DN33	14 B3	Wilton Rd. DN36	18 B1
Walnut Cres. DN35	11 B7	Wimborn Av. DN34	8 B6
Waltham Rd. DN33	16 D1	Winchcombe Av. DN34	13 G2
Walton Gro. DN33	14 C3	Winchester Av. DN33	14 A3
Ward St. DN35	10 A2	Windermere Av. DN33	16 C2
Wardall St. DN35	10 D4	Windermere Cres. DN36	18 C1
Warneford Rd. DN35	10 B2	Windlesham Av. DN33	16 B2
Warwick Av. DN33	14 A3	Windsor Rd. DN35	11 A5
Warwick Rd. DN35	11 B5	Wingate Par. DN37	7 G4
Waterside Dri. DN31	4 A2	Wingate Rd. DN37	7 F4
Watford Av. DN34	14 A2	Winn Ct. DN35	10 C4
Watkin St Nth. DN31	8 D4	Winslow Gro. DN34	14 A2
Watkin St Sth. DN31	8 D4	Winston Av. DN34	8 B6
Wayside Dri. DN36	17 G2	Winthorpe Rd. DN33	14 C4
Weekes Rd. DN35	11 D6	Wintringham Rd. DN32	9 E6
Weelsby Av. DN32	15 E2	Wirral Av. DN34	13 H2
Weelsby Gro. DN32	15 E2	Withern Rd. DN33	14 A4
Weelsby Rd. DN32	14 D2	Woad La. DN37	7 G3
Weelsby St. DN32	9 G5	Wold View. DN36	19 F5
Weelsby St. Sth. DN32	9 G5	Wollaston Rd. DN34	10 C4
Weelsby Vw. DN36	17 H1	Womersley Rd. DN31	9 G3
Welbeck Pl. DN34	13 H2	Wood Clo. DN33	16 D2
Welbeck Rd. DN34	13 G2	Wood St. DN32	4 E1
Welbeck Rd. DN35	11 A5	Woodfield Clo. DN36	18 D2
Welholme Av. DN32	14 D1	Woodhall Dri. DN37	16 A5
Welholme Rd. DN32	14 D1	Woodland Wk. DN35	11 C8
Well Vale. DN33	16 C1	Woodrow Pk. DN33	14 D5
Welland Av. DN34	13 H2	Woodsley Av. DN35	11 C5

Wootton Rd. DN33	14 B3		
Worcester Av. DN34	14 A2		
Worlaby Av. DN33	14 B6		
Worlaby Rd. DN33	16 B1		
Worsley Clo. DN36	19 F5		
Wragby St. DN32	4 F3		
Wray Clo. DN37	16 A5		
Wren Clo. DN37	6 B3		
Wroxham Av. DN34	13 G2		
Wybers Way. DN37	7 F5		
Wymark Vw. DN33	14 A4		
Wyndham Rd. DN36	17 G3		
Yarborough Dri. DN31	4 A2		
Yarborough Rd. DN34	8 A6		
Yardley Way. DN34	13 F2		
Yarorough Clo. DN36	19 F5		
Yarra Rd. DN35	10 D4		
Yarrow Rd. DN34	7 G6		
York Pl. DN35	11 A5		
York St. DN31	4 A1		
Young Pl. DN35	9 H5		

IMMINGHAM

Ainsworth Rd. DN40	5 B2		
Aire Clo. DN40	5 B3		
Alden Clo. DN40	5 C2		
Alderney Way. DN40	5 C4		
Allerton Dri. DN40	5 C2		
Ancholme Av. DN40	5 A3		
Anglesey Dri. DN40	5 C4		
Arran Clo. DN40	5 D4		
Ash Tree Clo. DN40	5 C1		
Atwood Clo. DN40	5 B1		
Balfour Pl. DN40	5 B2		
Barnard Wk. DN40	5 D3		
Battery St. DN40	5 D2		
Beechwood Av. DN40	5 C2		
Birkdale Dri. DN40	5 D1		
Blair Wk. DN40	5 E3		
Blossom Way. DN40	5 B3		
Bluestone La. DN40	5 B2		
Bowman Wk. DN40	5 B3		
Bradford Rd. DN40	5 B2		
Brewster Av. DN40	5 D3		
Calder Clo. DN40	5 A3		
Carver Rd. DN40	5 D3		
Cedar Clo. DN40	5 C1		
Chestnut Av. DN40	5 E2		
Chilton Clo. DN40	5 B2		
Church La. DN40	5 B1		
Clarence Clo. DN40	5 B3		
Cleveland Clo. DN40	5 A2		
Clyfton Cres. DN40	5 B2		
Collier Rd. DN40	5 D3		
Copse Clo. DN40	5 C1		
Corfe Wk. DN40	5 E3		
Craik Hill Av. DN40	5 C3		
Cushman Cres. DN40	5 C3		
Deane Rd. DN40	5 D2		
Dunster Wk. DN40	5 E3		
Eaton Rd. DN40	5 D2		
Fairisle Rise. DN40	5 D4		
Ferndown Dri. DN40	5 D1		
Green La. DN40	5 B2		
Guernsey Gro. DN40	5 C4		
Habrough Rd. DN40	5 A3		
Hadleigh Rd. DN40	5 D3		
Hamish Wk. DN40	5 B3		
Harlech Wk. DN40	5 D3		
Hawthorn Av. DN40	5 E2		
Hazel Croft. DN40	5 A2		
Helen Cres. DN40	5 A2		
Highfield Av. DN40	5 B3		
Highland Tarn. DN40	5 B3		
Hinkley Dri. DN40	5 B1		
Holbeck Pl. DN40	5 B1		
Hollingsworth Av. DN40	5 B2		
Hoylake Dri. DN40	5 D1		
Humberville Rd. DN40	5 D2		
Hume Brae. DN40	5 B3		

INDUSTRIAL ESTATES:

Pelham Ind Est. DN40	5 D1		
Ings La. DN40	5 D2		
Jackson Mews. DN40	5 A2		
James Way. DN40	5 B3		
Japonica Hill. DN40	5 C3		
Jasmine Way. DN40	5 C3		
Kendal Rd. DN40	5 E3		
Kings Rd. DN40	5 E2		
Kinloch Way. DN40	5 B3		
Kishorn Ct. DN40	5 B3		
Langley Wk. DN40	5 D3		
Lansdown Rd. DN40	5 B2		
Larch Clo. DN40	5 E2		
Leyden Clo. DN40	5 B2		
Lindum Av. DN40	5 B3		
Lulworth Wk. DN40	5 D3		
Lundy Ct. DN40	5 C4		
Lydford Rd. DN40	5 D3		
Lydia Ct. DN40	5 A2		
Magnolia Rise. DN40	5 C3		
Maiden Clo. DN40	5 A2		
Manby Rd. DN40	5 D1		
Maple Gro. DN40	5 C1		
Margaret St. DN40	5 D2		
Mayflower Av. DN40	5 C3		
McKenzie Pl. DN40	5 B3		
Middleplatt Rd. DN40	5 E1		
Mill La. DN40	5 A2		
Millhouse Rise. DN40	5 A2		
Morton Clo. DN40	5 B2		
Muirfield Ct. DN40	5 D2		
Muirfield Croft. DN40	5 D2		
Mull Way. DN40	5 C4		
Newark Wk. DN40	5 D3		
Newport Wk. DN40	5 D3		
Oakham Wk. DN40	5 E3		
Oaklands Rd. DN40	5 C1		
Oban Ct. DN40	5 B3		
Orkney Pl. DN40	5 D3		
Paddock Clo. DN40	5 C3		
Pamela Clo. DN40	5 D2		
Pamela Rd. DN40	5 D2		
Park Clo. DN40	5 C2		
Pelham Ind Est. DN40	5 D1		
Pelham Rd. DN40	5 B3		
Pennine Clo. DN40	5 A2		
Perth Way. DN40	5 B4		
Pilgrim Av. DN40	5 C3		
Pilgrims Way. DN40	5 A2		
Princess St. DN40	5 C2		
Robert Clo. DN40	5 B2		
Rose Gdns. DN40	5 C2		
Roundway. DN40	5 C3		
Roval Dri. DN40	5 A2		
Sackville Clo. DN40	5 D2		
Sackville Rd. DN40	5 D2		
St Andrews La. DN40	5 B1		
St Andrews Way. DN40	5 A2		
Shetland Way. DN40	5 C4		
Somerton Rd. DN40	5 E3		
Sonia Crest. DN40	5 B2		
Spinney Clo. DN40	5 C2		
Spring St. DN40	5 D2		
Stainton Dri. DN40	5 B2		
Stallingborough Rd. DN40	5 B3		
Standish La. DN40	5 B1		
Steeping Dri. DN40	5 A3		
Sunningdale Dri. DN40	5 D1		
Talbot Rd. DN40	5 D2		
Thornbury Rd. DN40	5 D3		
Thornton Pl. DN40	5 C3		
Trenchard Clo. DN40	5 E2		
Tummel Ct. DN40	5 B3		
Valda Vale. DN40	5 B2		
Viking Clo. DN40	5 A2		
Washdyke La. DN40	5 C1		
Waterworks St. DN40	5 E2		
Weston Gro. DN40	5 B1		
Winslow Dri. DN40	5 B2		
Woodlands Av. DN40	5 C1		
Worsley Clo. DN40	5 D2		
Worsley Rd. DN40	5 D2		